LIFE STORY

BUTTERFLY

MICHAEL CHINERY

Photography by
Barrie Watts

Illustrated by
Helen Senior

Troll Associates

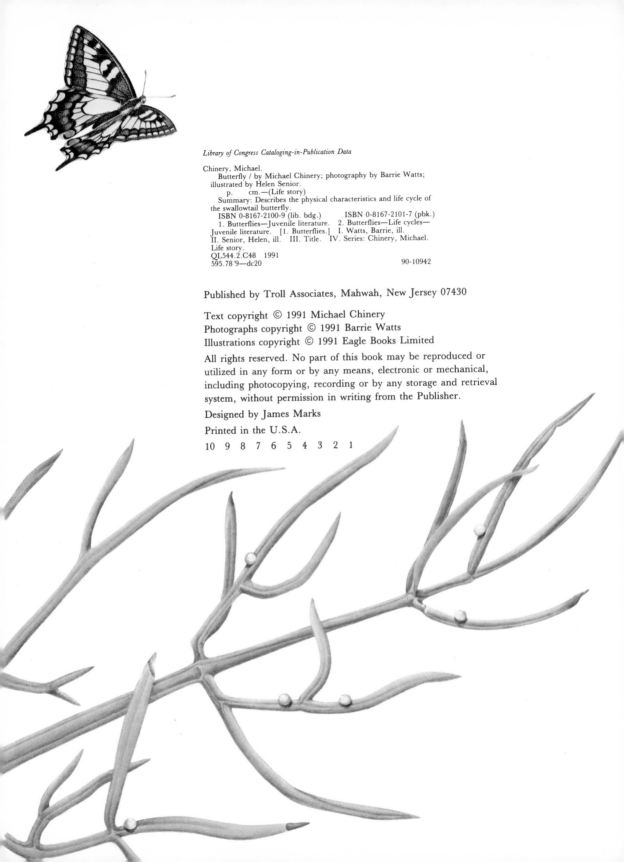

Library of Congress Cataloging-in-Publication Data

Chinery, Michael.
    Butterfly / by Michael Chinery; photography by Barrie Watts;
illustrated by Helen Senior.
        p.   cm.—(Life story)
    Summary: Describes the physical characteristics and life cycle of
the swallowtail butterfly.
    ISBN 0-8167-2100-9 (lib. bdg.)   ISBN 0-8167-2101-7 (pbk.)
    1. Butterflies—Juvenile literature.   2. Butterflies—Life cycles—
Juvenile literature.   [1. Butterflies.]   I. Watts, Barrie, ill.
II. Senior, Helen, ill.   III. Title.   IV. Series: Chinery, Michael.
Life story.
QL544.2.C48 1991
595.78'9—dc20   90-10942

Published by Troll Associates, Mahwah, New Jersey 07430

Designed by James Marks

Printed in the U.S.A.

10 9 8 7 6 5 4 3 2 1

INTRODUCTION

A caterpillar doesn't look anything like a butterfly. It doesn't have wings and it spends all day munching leaves instead of sipping nectar from the flowers. But a caterpillar does turn into a butterfly. This book will tell you how this happens by showing each change the caterpillar goes through to become a butterfly.

This beautiful butterfly is called a swallowtail. The streamers at the back of its wings look like the tail of a swallow. The butterfly you can see here is looking for somewhere to lay the eggs that are swelling inside her body.

To make sure she has chosen the right kind of plant, she taps it and sniffs it with her feelers. She also tastes it by stamping her feet on it. If she lays her eggs on the wrong plant, her babies will starve.

This swallowtail has found the right kind of plant for her eggs. It is a fennel plant. Now the butterfly is pushing an egg out from the end of her body and sticking it firmly to the fennel leaf.

   She will lay about 100 eggs, but not all in one place. She spreads them out, one by one, all over the fennel plants in the area. She is making sure that the caterpillars that come out of the eggs will have plenty to eat.

Here is a swallowtail's egg a few days after it was laid. It is not much bigger than the head of a pin. Swallowtails' eggs are pale yellow when they are laid, but they soon turn brown, then gray.

Big changes are taking place inside the egg. At first it is full of liquid that looks like soup. But somewhere in that liquid a tiny caterpillar is starting to grow. After about seven days the caterpillar almost fills the egg. Its black head can be seen through the shell. The egg is now ready to hatch.

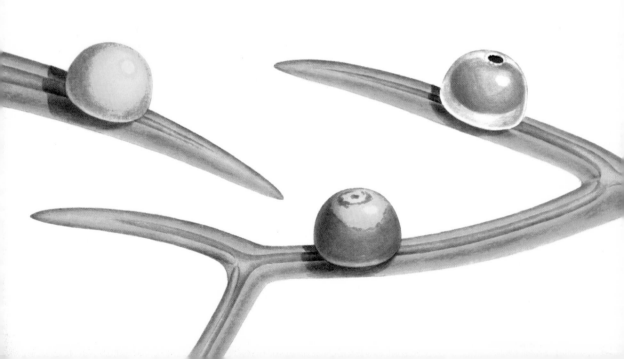

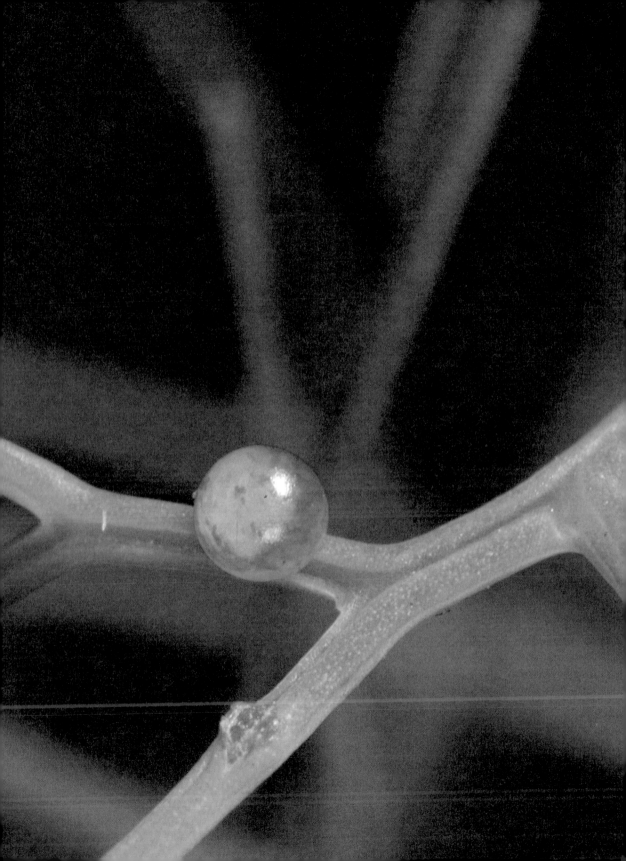

The tiny caterpillar already has tough
jaws. It nibbles a hole in the eggshell
and pokes its head out. After a short
rest, it makes the hole bigger and crawls
out of the egg.

　　The caterpillar in the photograph is
hungry, so it starts to eat its eggshell.
The first meal is very important,
because the eggshell contains minerals
the caterpillar needs. But it won't eat all
of the shell. Soon it will start to feed on
the fennel leaves.

10

Caterpillars have many enemies. But the young swallowtail caterpillar is protected because it looks like a bird dropping. Birds leave these caterpillars alone, although spiders eat them. If it can avoid all its enemies, the caterpillar feeds almost nonstop for two or three days. It grows quickly and its skin gets very tight.

The caterpillar has to stop feeding, and it sits quietly for a few hours. Then its skin splits open. Underneath the old skin, a new, looser skin has already grown. The caterpillar wriggles out of its old skin and soon starts eating again.

The swallowtail caterpillar changes its skin four times during its life. After the third change, it becomes green with orange and black markings.

It continues to munch the fennel leaves, and it may also climb up to eat the flowers. The caterpillar clings tightly to the stem with its ten stumpy back legs. It uses six slender legs at the front to push the food into its mouth.

When the caterpillar is frightened, it pushes out a bright orange, Y-shaped blob just behind its head. This gives out a strong smell and frightens some of the caterpillar's enemies away. But birds eat quite a lot of plump caterpillars when they are at this stage of their lives.

After four weeks or so, the caterpillar is about two inches long and a bit thicker than a pencil. It is now ready for its amazing change into an adult butterfly. The caterpillar fixes a pad of silk to a thick, strong stem and clings to it with its back legs. Then it fixes another silk pad a little higher up the stem. By bending its head back and moving it from side to side, it spins a silken safety belt around itself. The belt is fixed to the second pad. The silk all comes from a gland near the caterpillar's mouth. Held in place by the belt, the caterpillar's body starts to shrink. The big change has begun.

The caterpillar stays very still after fixing its safety belt. But after a couple of days it starts to wriggle and its skin splits open. After a few more wriggles, the old caterpillar skin is shrugged off.

The animal has entered the chrysalis stage of its life. The chrysalis does not feed or move about, but inside it the caterpillar's body is turning into the body of a beautiful butterfly. You can already see the outlines of the wings on the chrysalis shell.

18

The new butterfly might be ready to leave its chrysalis after about three weeks, but many swallowtails stay in the chrysalis stage all through the winter. When all is ready, the chrysalis gets very thin and you can see the wing colors through it.

Then the shell splits and the new butterfly struggles out, as you can see in the photograph. This may take only a few seconds, or it may take several minutes. The butterfly can't fly yet because its wings are soft and crumpled. It must hold on tightly to the stem with its feet while it unfolds its wings.

Most new butterflies climb toward the tops of the plants before they start to unfold their wings. This one is happy to cling to its old chrysalis. The wings are slowly unfolding as the blood is pumped along the veins in them.

After about half an hour, all the wrinkles will have disappeared and the wings will be smooth and flat, as in the drawing below. The wing tip is the last part to straighten out.

This swallowtail's wings have reached their full size and you can see the veins that carry the blood through them. But the wings are still very soft and the butterfly can't fly yet. It must hang with its wings like this for an hour or two until they are hard and dry.

It will then open its wings and bask in the sunshine to warm up its muscles. Only then is the butterfly ready for the big moment – its first flight.

24

The new swallowtail uses its beautiful wings to float and glide over the fields. Every now and then it stops to drink sweet nectar from the flowers. When it lands on a flower, the butterfly uncoils its hairlike tongue and pushes it deep into the flower, to reach the nectar. The tongue is hollow, and the butterfly uses it like a drinking straw to suck up the nectar.

Although the original butterfly may have laid 100 eggs, only two or three of them grow to be new butterflies. All the rest of them are eaten by birds or other enemies at some stage of their life story.

Male butterflies spend a lot of time flying slowly over the fields, but each one has a favorite bush or patch of flowers to which it returns again and again. Several males may gather at the same place. When a female arrives, one of the males will fly off with her. They flutter around each other and often spiral up into the air. The pair in the photograph have returned to the plant to mate. The female is a little bigger and fatter than the male because her body is full of eggs. After mating, she goes off to lay her eggs. She usually dies within a couple of weeks, but her new family is on its way.

Fascinating facts

The world's largest butterfly is Queen Alexandra's birdwing, which lives in New Guinea and neighboring islands. Its wings can measure over eleven inches.

The world's smallest butterfly is the dwarf blue. It lives in South Africa and its wings are only about half an inch across.

The caterpillars of some blue butterflies grow up in ants' nests, where they actually eat the ants' grubs.

The European brimstone is one of the longest-lived butterflies. It flies from June until the fall and then goes into a long sleep until March. It flies around for another three months when it wakes up, and dies just before the new generation appears, so it lives for about a year.

Monarch butterflies in North America fly thousands of miles in the fall to spend winter resting in trees and bushes in Mexico and southern parts of the United States.

The dwarf blue, seen (*left*) from above and (*right*) from below.

A butterfly's colors are produced by thousands of tiny, overlapping scales fixed to its wings. These scales come off easily if you rub the wings with a finger.

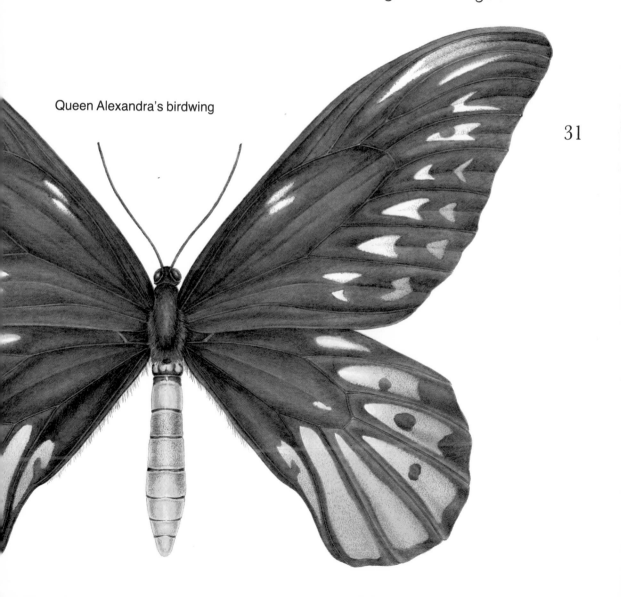

Queen Alexandra's birdwing

Index